Back to Basics

By Suzanne Massee

This book is copyright. Apart from any fair dealing for the purpose of private study, research, criticism or review, as permitted under the Copyright Act, no part may be reproduced by any process without prior permission of Suzanne Massee.

© Suzanne Massee 2009

Designed by: Tigerzi Design

ISBN978-0-6483675-0-5 Paperback

ISBN 978-0-648-3420-3-8 Hardcover
2nd edition 2018

Dedicated to the Universe

May we acquire a wealth of knowledge and love of what Mother Nature has provided in abundance around our universe.

May the sleeping inner consciousness, your very own all-knowing of the spirit within, be awakened to concentration of thought, and give birth to reality - a reality that needs no energy: you are the energy.

It awakens the greatest teacher of all: "The Self".

Back to Basics

"Back to Basics" is not intended to replace medical advice. Consult your health-care professional for specific medical conditions and inform your health-care professionals of treatments you are taking.

All due and reasonable care has been taken in the preparation of this book; but neither the writer nor editor can accept responsibility for any consequence of the use or misuse of information contained within.

"Back to Basics" is intended to help you gain a greater knowledge and understanding of traditional plant remedies.

Contents

Introduction	6
Culinary Herbs and Uses	8
Suggested Uses	10
Herbal Teas	14
Herbal Butters	15
Herbal Salts	16
Herbal Oils	17
Herbal Vinegars	18
Soups	21
Mains	25
Baking	33
Sweets	41
Novelty Confectionery	47
Condiments and Hints	53
Cheese Products	61
Medicinal	69
Definition of First Aid Terms	74
Suggested First Aid	76
Herbal Cosmetics	86
Skin Cleansers	88
Household Cleaning Alternatives	91
Plants that Purify the Air	96
In the Garden	97
Children's Section	98
Glossary of Herbs in this Book	101
Conversion Chart	107
Author's Note	108

Tarragon

Introduction

I have been interested in cooking and herbalism from an early age.

To prepare simple foods with little effort is a culinary delight that need not involve any great time or expense - you certainly do not need to slave in the kitchen to produce outstanding dishes.

I once owned a restaurant which, when it had just opened, was entered into the Montana Wine and Food Challenge; it became the overall winner for the Nelson, Marlborough, and West Coast region! As well, I have created and produced preserves throughout New Zealand.

Food is an enjoyable basis for interaction when shared with friends; it's good to share knowledge about what is grown and produced in our own space.

I have accumulated years of recipes and knowledge that I want to see passed on to our children and children's children before all this knowledge is lost. Daily we watch the global advance of commercial packet foods, fast food outlets ... even household cleaners!

I find it extremely sad to see so much packet food being consumed with so little knowledge of what is being ingested and – eventually - washed down into our Planet Earth. Think of the savings that could be achieved by going "Back to Basics". Not only this: think about what you are consuming.

I have incorporated fun confectionery food that can be made with children, for them to enjoy, like candy-coated popcorn or homemade chocolate.

Most recipes are easily made so all the family can partake; some of the recipes are good for away-from-home students on a budget.

I love to cook with natural ingredients that are grown in abundance around Mother Earth, together with our very own herbs and weeds.

Herbs are a natural flavoursome ingredient, which grow in pots or can be purchased dry. I implore you all to grow your own herbs; there is nothing nicer than adding them to your salads and stocks to give them their own natural character, rather than some salt-infused flavour from the supermarket.

If you have a larger garden leave some plants to go to seed. Either gather and save the seeds or just let them lie where they fall; they'll germinate next spring.

I have incorporated a list of culinary herbs to help guide you in your herb use. I have also added a list of my favourite weeds; these probably grow in abundance in your garden, too. We call these plants weeds, but do remember they reproduce in abundance and grow pest-free year in and year out. I implore you to think about it: the weeds you are getting rid of may very well have more minerals and vitamins than green vegetables bought at a grocer. My list contains a few of my favourite weeds, for consumption and for medicinal use.

Chickweed

Culinary Herbs and uses

What could be more natural than to go out into the garden and pick nature's own flavours? There is nothing more satisfying than adding these ingredients to the pot: the natural vitamins and minerals clean the soul, and their aromas fill the air.

Due to the dominance of the supermarket, and easily-obtained prescription medicines, a wealth of knowledge has been lost - however we are now seeing new attitudes evolving. We are becoming more aware of what we are ingesting; natural medicines and foods are being rediscovered. These plants do not take up much room and can grow in pots, are very pest-resistant, and love to be trimmed. What could be better than having flavoursome, chemical-free plants in your own home-grown supermarket?

The herbs used are available in most gardens; some herbs are there all year round and can see you through the winter months. As you will see, most herbs can be used for most dishes: once you've identified what types of herbs to use, begin with small quantities.

My favourite salad or vegetable weed is **Chickweed** (Stellaria Media). Chickweed is packed full of nutrition and grows everywhere. It contains vitamins A, B, B1, B2, B12, C, D and minerals copper, iron, calcium, sodium, potassium, silica, manganese, phosphorus and zinc. WOW! Why would you ever weed this plant? Use it raw to give your salads a different texture. Or you could blanch it – chopped or left whole - as you would spinach, and fold it into an omelette.

To replace spinach use **Fat Hen** (Chenopodium album) also known as goosefoot, lamb's quarters, bacon weed, dirty Dick - to list a few of its names. But aside from all its names it is power-packed with nourishment: more B1 and B2, protein and iron, than raw cabbage.

When shoots are young I use the whole plant; from mature plants I use the leaves only. You need to pick a lot though, as it reduces to a quarter of its original bulk.

Either blanch like spinach, or fry in a little butter and oil.

Add salt, pepper and/or nutmeg.

Fat Hen

Cleaver (Galium aparine), also called woodruff or bed straw is rich in silica: very good for your nails. It is a tonic for the lymph system as it strengthens lymphatic circulation.

It is used to treat urinary, cystitis and ulcer problems.

It has strong diuretic and anti-cancer properties.

Gather a bundle of cleaver and put it into a large jug. Fill it with cold water, and leave to sit overnight. Drink it the next day; the taste is not unlike cucumber.

Again, the soft shoots can be added to salads or blanched just like spinach.

Cleaver

Suggested Uses

Bouquet Garni

Parsley	2 sprigs
Thyme	1 sprig
Bay leaf	1 leaf
Sage	1 sprig
Rosemary	1 sprig
Lovage	1 sprig

Use for soups, sauces, stocks, casseroles.

These are only suggestions; feel free to add to or delete from this list.

Bouquet Garni

Salads

Chervil, Chives, Garlic Chives and flowers, Dill, Lemon Balm, Marjoram, Mint, Parsley, Salad Burnet, Savory, French Sorrel, Sheep Sorrel, Chickweed, Nasturtium leaves and flowers, Borage flowers, Oregano, Basil, Coriander.

Eggs

Basil, Tarragon, Chervil, Parsley, Chives, Dill, Marjoram, Oregano.

Sauces

Chervil, Chives, Dill, Parsley, Marjoram, Tarragon.

Basil

Fish

Tarragon, Basil, Dill, Chervil, Chives, Fennel, Lemon Balm, Lemon Thyme, Parsley, Sage, Lovage, Oregano.

Poultry

Chicken: Basil, Bay, Rosemary, Lovage, Tarragon, Thyme, Marjoram, Sage.

Stuffing: Marjoram, Basil, Oregano, Rosemary, Sage, Tarragon, Thyme.

Meats

Beef: Rosemary, Sage, Bay, Thyme, Lovage, Horseradish.

Lamb: Dill, Mint, Sage, Rosemary, Lovage.

Casseroles: Mixture of the above for a Bouquet Garni.

Vegetables

Avocado: Dill, Marjoram, Tarragon, Coriander.

Asparagus: Chervil, Chives, Lemon Balm, Dill, Salad Burnet, Tarragon.

Beans: Dill, Marjoram, Oregano, Rosemary, Savory, Tarragon, Thyme.

Brussels Sprouts: Dill, Sage, Savory.

Cabbage: Caraway, Dill seed or leaves, Fennel, Mint, Tarragon.

Carrots: Basil, Chervil, Dill, Marjoram, Oregano, Parsley, Sage, Thyme, Savory.

Cauliflower: Chives, Dill, Rosemary, Fennel.

Celeriac: Tarragon

Mushrooms:	Dill, Basil, Marjoram, Thyme, Tarragon, Savory, Rosemary, Salad Burnet.
Onions:	Marjoram, Oregano, Sage, Tarragon, Thyme.
Peas:	Basil, Mint, Marjoram, Rosemary, Sage, Savory, Chervil.
Potatoes:	Chives, Dill, Marjoram, Mint, Parsley, Savory; Rosemary and Thyme with roast potatoes.
Spinach:	Chervil, Marjoram, Oregano, Mint, Rosemary, Sorrel, Tarragon.
Tomato:	Basil, Chervil, Dill, Marjoram, Oregano, Savory, Tarragon.
Turnips:	Dill, Marjoram, Savory.
Zucchini / Courgette:	Basil, Dill, Marjoram, Mint, Rosemary, Tarragon.

Herbs for Desserts and Fruit Punches:

Angelica:	Chop the stems finely and add to apples, berries and fruit salad.
Borage Flowers:	In fruit salads, jellies and fruit punches.
Elderberry:	Flowers for elderberry wine, and in jellies.
Calendula:	Petals in custards, jellies and ice cream.
Lemon Balm:	Rhubarb, apples, oranges, peaches, berries, fruit salads, homemade sorbets and ice creams.

Elderberry

Calendula

Lemon Verbena: Flavours jellies, custards, summer drinks and salad dressings.

Peppermint: In fruit salads, sorbets and fruit punch.

Edible Petals and Flowers:

Turn those jellies, punches and summer salads into a colourful and tasty delight by using petals and flowers.

Petals: Of rose, day lily, calendula, gladiola.

Flowers: Borage, rosemary, violet, lemon thyme, nasturtium, elderflowers, chives, carnations, thyme, oregano, marjoram, mint, sage, lemon verbena, lavender, pansy, courgette, pelargoniums, dill, mustard and mallow (the young leaves of mallow are also edible and when blanched become a delicate green).

Herbal Teas

Place fresh herbs into a coffee plunger or cup, pour boiling water over them, and leave to infuse for 5 minutes.

Remove the fresh herbs from the cup if you wish and then enjoy.

Ideal herbs to use:

Mint, Chamomile, Lemon Verbena, Lemon Balm, Dandelion, Sage, Ginger, Gingko, Parsley.

Herbal Butters

These add real excitement to everyday dishes. Use them on baked and boiled vegetables; spread them on meat before grilling - or just before serving. Make up any combination - just have fun.

To make herbal butters, soften butter, add chopped herbs, and combine with a fork.

Make fancy piped swirls, or chill butter in a log and cut into slices or wedges.

Suggested Herbal Butter Combinations:

Calendula Petals and Thyme

Parsley and Chopped Garlic

Chives and Parsley

Mint Butter: This is great with grilled meat and potatoes, or spread on French bread sticks.

Lemon Verbena Leaves: Spread this on fish and toast, grilled meat or potatoes.

Basil Butter: Place a dollop onto grilled tomatoes, fish or eggs.

Herbal Salt Culinary

Make your own herbal salts to apply to your own menu.

In a small container add 2 tablespoons of salt, and add spices and dried herbs to taste (start with a teaspoon of spices or herbs and add more if required for more intense flavour).

Suggested Seasoning Salts:

Dried Lemon Peel: Make by peeling a lemon, or use a lemon zester. Place the lemon zest or peel on an oven tray and dry in the oven on a low heat, or put out in the sun to dry. Store dried peel in a container.

Lemon Pepper: 1 teaspoon salt, 1 teaspoon chopped dried lemon peel/zest, ½ teaspoon ground black pepper, and a large pinch white pepper. Use on fish and chicken.

Try one teaspoon each of dried thyme, sage and rosemary and 2 teaspoons of salt. Combine and use on grilled meats and roast vegetables. Wonderful on kumara, potato and pumpkin roast.

Seasoning ratio: 6 teaspoons salt and 1 teaspoon white pepper; this is the standard blend in use in most bakeries to season meat pie fillings. Save in a container and season to taste.

Herbal Oils

Herbal oils are especially delicious in cooking and an excellent way to preserve fresh herbs like basil when out of season.

It is important to use dry herbs, as any water from fresh herbs can cause mould.

Take 1/2 cup of olive oil, vegetable oil or rice bran oil. Hard pack 1 cup of fresh herbs, and process in the blender with the oil.

Alternatively, finely chop the herbs, and add to the oil. Bottle.

To store fresh herb oil, refrigerate or freeze. In the case of basil oil, freezing is recommended.

Gourmet herbal oils:

Place into a plain or fancy bottle 6 peppercorns, 6 dried chillies, garlic, olives and sundried tomatoes (optional)

Fill with olive oil, vegetable oil or rice bran oil. Leave in a cool dark place for between a week and a month, to infuse.

Flavoured oils are excellent as a dip with breads, or for grilling, basting and frying.

Herbs to use for gourmet oils

For savoury use: Basil, garlic, fennel, marjoram, mint, rosemary, tarragon, thyme, savory.

For sweet use: Lavender, lemon verbena, rose petals.

Herbal Vinegars

Herbal vinegars are flavoured vinegars for use in salad dressings, marinades, gravies and sauces or for adding to poached-egg water.

To make tarragon vinegar, place in a plain or fancy bottle peppercorns, dried or fresh chilli, mustard seeds and a large sprig of fresh tarragon.

Use your imagination and create many other interesting flavours.

Herbs for Vinegars

Basil, Chervil, Dill, Fennel, Garlic, Lemon Balm, Marjoram, Mint, Rosemary, Savory, Thyme.

Flowers for Vinegars

Carnations, Clover, Elderflowers, Lavender, Nasturtiums,

Rose petals, Rosemary flowers, Thyme flowers and sweet Violets.

Recipes

These dishes are very easy to make; they do not involve a lot of time or ingredients. They look and taste good and can be made by using just one pot or pan.

Soups

Mushroom Soup with Fresh Thyme

Serves 2-4

250g mushrooms

75g butter

2 cloves garlic, crushed

1 onion, chopped

2 tablespoons flour

1 teaspoon fresh thyme or lemon thyme

2 ½ cups chicken stock or milk

Salt

1 teaspoon black pepper

150g sour cream

Grated cheese and chopped thyme or parsley to garnish

Slice mushrooms. Fry butter with garlic and onions and cook until soft. Add mushrooms, stir and cook over medium heat for 5 minutes. Add flour and thyme, stir through the butter and cook through for one minute, then add stock or milk and salt and pepper. Bring to the boil and reduce heat and simmer for 15 mins.

Take off heat and stir in sour cream, reserving a little for garnish. Garnish with grated cheese and thyme and reserved sour cream.

Variation puree soup in a processor for a thick creamy version. Try adding crumbled blue cheese and slices of fresh mushrooms, or a raw oyster.

Lentil and Coriander Soup

Serves 2-4

1 tablespoon vegetable oil

1 large onion, chopped

110gms split red lentils

570mls tomato juice - or 1 tin of whole peeled tomatoes for chunky-style soup.

300ml water

Salt and pepper

1 tablespoon ground coriander seeds

1 tablespoon chopped fresh coriander

Heat the oil in a saucepan and sauté the onion for 5 minutes. Add lentils and sauté for a few minutes.

Stir in whole or juiced tomatoes, water, seasoning and ground coriander. Bring to the boil and simmer 20 minutes, stirring a few times to stop the lentils sticking to the pot. Serve hot, sprinkled with the chopped coriander.

Curried Zucchini Soup

This soup is wonderful for those zucchini that have bolted away into marrows. Freeze marrows de-seeded and chopped into chunks and be ready to make this hearty soup on winter days.

2 onions chopped

2 tablespoons vegetable oil

4 garlic cloves, chopped

2 teaspoons grated ginger

2 teaspoons curry powder

1 ½ litres water or stock

4 medium potatoes, chopped

2 kg zucchini or marrow, chopped

3 teaspoons salt

Sauté the onions with the vegetable oil, add garlic, ginger, curry powder, salt, water or stock, potatoes and zucchini. Bring to the boil and simmer. When cooked, mix in the blender or use a food wand stick.

Return to low heat and add

4 teaspoons chopped fresh coriander

2 cups milk

1½ cups yoghurt

2 tablespoons vinegar

Heat through. Season to taste.

Mains

Beef Stroganoff

Serves 4

1kg beef Weiner schnitzel sliced into finger size pieces.

125g butter

1 tablespoon chopped onion

Salt and pepper

250g sliced mushrooms

300ml sour cream

Large pinch Spanish smoked paprika

Using half the butter sauté the sliced mushrooms until cooked; remove from the pan and put into a bowl.

Using the same frypan sauté the onions in the remaining half of the butter and add them to the bowl of mushrooms.

Brown the Weiner schnitzel in the pan; add the sautéed mushrooms and onions. Stir in the smoked paprika, fold in the sour cream, and add salt and pepper to taste.

Serve with new potatoes, pasta or rice and salad.

Tomato Sauce for Pasta

2 tins whole peeled tomatoes

2 onions, chopped

2 garlic cloves, chopped

1 teaspoon dried basil or 1 tablespoon chopped fresh basil

1 teaspoon dried oregano or 1 tablespoon chopped fresh oregano

1 teaspoon sugar (brings out the flavour in tomatoes)

Salt/pepper to taste

½ teaspoon ground cloves

Wine, stock or ½ cup water to cover onions and garlic

Fry the onions and garlic until soft. Add the wine, stock or water to deglaze bottom of pan. Reduce liquid by a third.

Add tomatoes, herbs, sugar, cloves.

Reduce liquid by a further third or until thickened.

Add salt and pepper to taste.

This sauce makes a chunky tomato sauce to put over cooked pasta.

With this sauce you can add zucchini, celery, bacon, salami, ham or broccoli, or any vegetable of choice. Heat veggies through in the tomato sauce until cooked.

Serve on pasta with grated or sliced parmesan or cheese and chopped fresh herbs, either basil or oregano.

Spicy Tomato Sauce Pasta

Serves 4

2 tablespoons oil

4 garlic cloves, crushed

1 large onion, chopped

2 tablespoons chopped parsley or basil

1 chilli, chopped or ½ teaspoon chilli powder

1 teaspoon sugar

2 tins whole peeled tomatoes

2 tablespoons chopped capers

6 anchovies chopped

1/2 cup olives

Sauté onion and garlic. Add chillies and tomatoes, bring to the boil and simmer 5 mins.

Add capers, anchovies, parsley or basil and olives. Season to taste, and simmer 5 mins.

Serve with cooked pasta topped with grated or shaved parmesan or grated cheese and garnished with basil, oregano or parsley.

Curry Dish with Powdered Spices and Tomato Paste

Serves 2

1 clove garlic chopped

1 onion, chopped

1 teaspoon curry powder

1 teaspoon turmeric

2 teaspoons tomato paste

Pepper/salt to taste

Half tin coconut cream

Stock or water - about 1 cup.

Fry onion and garlic until soft, add spices and tomato paste, fry lightly to bring out the flavours of the spices - about 1 minute - add stock or water, scrape the bottom of the pan to get all the lovely cooking juices off the bottom, and add coconut cream.

Heat through and cook for about 5-10 mins.

To this sauce you can add fish, chicken or vegetables to poach. When cooked, serve with cooked rice.

Variation: you can use a whole tin of coconut cream for more in-depth coconut flavour. This will serve 4 people.

Creamy Curry Sauce for Chicken, Vegetarian and Seafood Dishes

Serves 4

1 tablespoon vegetable oil

1 tablespoons chopped or grated ginger

2 cloves garlic, crushed

2 small onions, chopped

2 whole fresh chillies - sliced with seeds - or ½ teaspoon dried whole chillies, chopped

1 red pepper, chopped

Coriander stalks and roots (use the leaves for the garnish)

2 lemon grass stalks or 1 kaffir lime leaf; if unavailable replace with sliced lime or lemon (it's not the same but will be an OK replacement).

Sauté the above ingredients in oil for 3 mins

Add 1 teaspoon turmeric and 1 tablespoon flour and blend.

Stir in slowly 1/2 litre of stock or water. Add 1 tin coconut cream, 1/2 tsp fish sauce. Season with salt and pepper; simmer about 10 mins.

To this sauce you can add fish, including salmon, shelled mussels or chicken, or vegetables to poach. Serve when cooked.

Instead of poaching you can fry to brown the meats or veggies and add to the sauce.

Garnish with chopped coriander, and for the fish dish, cooked mussels in their opened shells.

Serve with rice or udon noodles.

Add basil to the chicken and vegetable dish.

Coriander to the fish dish

Thai Fish Cakes

500g fish fillets

2 small chillies

2 cloves garlic

Lemon grass (optional)

2 tablespoons coriander leaves

1 tablespoon fish sauce

1 egg

¼ cup coconut milk

Process in blender, make into patties and chill.

Fry for about 2 minutes each side; don't over-cook.

Students' Hearty 2-minute Noodles

Serves 1 to 2 depending on how many vegetables are added.

I do not usually advocate packet food but on a cost/benefit ratio this does make a complete hearty meal.

1 onion, chopped

2 cloves garlic, chopped

A piece of ginger the size of a garlic clove, chopped.

1 small carrot, sliced

1 celery stick, sliced

3 mushrooms, sliced

Cabbage portion, sliced.

Bean Sprouts

1 packet 2-minute noodles

Sauté onions, ginger and garlic in a wok or fry pan. Add carrots, celery and mushrooms and stir-fry - adding spoonfuls of hot water to steam vegetables - for 2 minutes. Break 2-minute noodles in half and place in pan. Add 1 cup of hot water, powdered sachet flavour and cabbage, then put the lid on and steam until the noodles are cooked. In a cup mix 1 to 2 teaspoons of cornflour in a little water, add to the pan and stir to thicken. Add soy sauce and enjoy.

Variations: Fry Wiener schnitzel, chicken or fish pieces after onions have been sautéed and then proceed with recipe.

Baking

Recipes can be altered to add honey instead of sugar.

Diabetics can replace sugar with Splenda.

(Using sugar alternatives creates a slightly denser cake and a shorter keeping quality.)

Pikelets

3 eggs

2 1/2 cups milk

1tsp vanilla essence

110 ml melted butter

1 1/2 tablespoons sugar

1 1/2 heaped tablespoons baking powder

3 cups flour

Put all ingredients into a food processor and whiz until the batter is smooth.

Let mixture rest for about 1 hour. Put a large spoon of pikelet mixture onto medium heat pan; it will bubble when it's time to turn over and cook the other side.

Serve in a stack with maple syrup and fresh fruit or

maple syrup, banana and crisp fried bacon.

Muffins

3 cups flour

1 cup sugar

4 tsp baking powder

Pinch of salt

In a large bowl, sift ingredients altogether and make a well.

Whisk in a small bowl:

2 eggs

1 cup milk

150 ml melted butter

Add this liquid to the dry ingredients. Fold the ingredients; do not over mix. Spoon into a muffin tin, using a large spoon so as not to over-work the ingredients

This is the base recipe; add fruit or chocolate into the centre of each muffin.

Or make combinations of:

¼ cup lemon verbena leaves chopped.

Lavender flowers (Lavendula Augustifolia) and white chocolate.

To make cocoa muffins replace two dessertspoons of flour with two tablespoons of cocoa powder. Bake 190c 20 to 30 minutes or until skewer comes out clean.

A tip for removing muffins: allow to cool slightly and then twist muffin out of pan.

Chocolate Cake

1½ cups water

1 cup raisins or dates

250g butter

1 cup sugar

½ teaspoon cinnamon

½ teaspoon cloves

3 heaped tablespoons cocoa

¼ teaspoon salt

1 teaspoon baking soda

1 teaspoon vanilla

2 cups flour

Put everything except baking soda, vanilla and flour into saucepan and bring to boil. Cook about 5 mins and leave to cool.

Dissolve soda into mixture, sift in flour and add vanilla to mixture; mix all ingredients.

Put mixture into a ring tin, bake 45 mins at 180c. or until skewer comes out clean.

This cake is very moist.

Serve with Ganache.

Chocolate Ganache

Melt 100g dark chocolate into ½ cup cream, mix well.

(There are no hard and fast rules here: add more or less cream to suit.)

The microwave is excellent for heating Ganache; stir often to avoid the chocolate burning.

By way of a change, chop half a hot fresh chilli and mix into the Ganache.

Or grind a star anise to a powder and add it to the mix.

Wholemeal Loaves

Makes 2 loaf tins

3 cups water

2 cups sugar

60g butter

375g sultanas

1 teaspoon mixed spice

1 teaspoon cinnamon

1 teaspoon ground cloves

Put all ingredients into a large pot and bring to the boil.

Take off heat. Leave to cool.

Add 4 cups flour, ¼ teaspoon salt, 2 teaspoons baking soda. Mix well.

Grease loaf tins and place greaseproof paper on the bottom of the tins.

Bake 160 degrees Celsius for 1 hour or until skewer comes out clean.

Anzac Biscuits

250g flour

300g sugar

2 cups coconut

2 cups rolled oats

200g butter

2 tablespoons golden syrup

1 teaspoon baking soda

Mix in a large bowl the flour, sugar, coconut, baking soda and rolled oats.

Melt the butter in a pot and add the golden syrup. Add to dry ingredients and mix; if mixture is a little too dry add some more melted butter.

Make into balls and flatten slightly.

Bake 350 degrees for 15 to 20 mins. I like to reduce heat and bake a little longer to completely dry out the biscuit.

Makes about 23 biscuits.

For a different flavour add 2 teaspoons of caraway seeds.

Kiwi Biscuit

450g butter

700g flour

350g sugar

4 teaspoons baking powder

4 tablespoons condensed milk

Pinch salt

2 teaspoons vanilla

Chocolate chips - up to a cup.

Cream butter and sugar and add dry ingredients.

Make into balls and flatten slightly, or roll into a log, cut into 1cm slices, and press slightly.

Bake 350 degrees for 15 to 20 mins. I like to reduce the heat and bake a little longer to completely dry out the biscuit.

Bake 180c for 10 to 20 mins

Makes about 40 large biscuits.

For a difference add Lavendula Augustifolia flowers and white chocolate,

or Calendula flower petals from 3 flower heads, plus 1 cup sultanas.

Coconut Ice Slice

Yummy pastry (on page 42)

Roll out pastry to a thickness of about 8mm, place in a slice dish, prick the base with a fork all over to prevent shrinkage, and bake for 15 to 20 minutes at 200 degrees Celsius or until golden brown.

Spread raspberry jam over base.

Coconut Ice:

1 tin condensed milk

350g softened butter

600g icing sugar

225g coconut

1 teaspoon vanilla essence

Place all ingredients into a blender and blend, spread mixture over the raspberry jam, sprinkle top with desiccated coconut. Leave to set in refrigerator. Cut into portions.

Variation: Make coconut ice, sprinkle desiccated coconut into a shallow pan, and place half the mixture into the pan. With the left over mixture add up to five drops of cochineal and blend in blender place this on top of the base mixture, sprinkle with desiccated coconut, chill and cut into portions.

Chocolate Mousse Decadence

3 eggs, separated

200g dark chocolate, melted

100ml cream, lightly whipped

Stir egg yolks into melted chocolate until well blended.

Whisk egg whites until stiff, fold into chocolate mixture until evenly blended. Fold in whipped cream and spoon into glasses to set.

Sweets

Quick Inexpensive Chocolate Sauce

½ cup icing sugar

1 tablespoon cocoa powder

2 teaspoons custard powder

1 cup milk

1 tablespoon butter

1 teaspoon vanilla essence.

Sift icing sugar, cocoa and custard powder. Mix in milk until smooth, then add butter and vanilla.

Heat uncovered in microwave for 4 minutes until bubbling, stirring several times; or heat on stove-top, stirring until it comes to the boil.

For a thicker sauce add more custard powder.

Delicious poured over ice-cream.

Make a banana split (split a banana in half, place on top of

Ice-cream and pour hot sauce over it.)

Serve with strawberries.

Serve on any pudding that requires a chocolate sauce.

Lactose-intolerant Ice-cream

2 cups strawberries

2 tablespoons lemon juice

1 cup sugar

2 egg whites

Beat altogether on high speed for 10 minutes. Freeze. This is a really delicious mousse ice-cream. Makes nearly 4 litres.

An option for the non-lactose-intolerant:

Fold in 1 bottle of whipped cream to the beaten egg mixture.

Use the left-over egg yolks to make the yummy pastry when you make the apple pie below.

Yummy Pastry

250g flour

60g caster sugar

Pinch salt

180g butter

2 egg yolks

Few drops water

In a food processor, combine the flour, sugar and salt, add butter, and process until it resembles breadcrumbs. Add egg yolks and water. Knead and cover. Refrigerate 1 hour.

Apple Pie

Roll out three-quarters of the pastry, place in a pie dish, prick the base with a fork all over to prevent shrinkage, and bake for about 10 minutes at 200 degrees Celsius. This is to partially cook the base, helping prevent it from becoming soggy.

Add partially-cooked drained apples to base and sprinkle with cinnamon. Roll out the rest of the pastry and place on top of the apples, glaze the top with a beaten egg or milk, sprinkle with sugar, and bake for a further 20 to 30 minutes until browned.

Or

Proceed with pre-baking pastry but instead of cooked apples, grate the apples - skin and all - and mix in 1 teaspoon cinnamon and 1 tablespoon sugar, and put that onto the base.

Roll out the rest of the pastry into pencil-shaped logs and create a lattice-top glaze. Proceed to bake as above.

Children's Favourite Ambrosia Marshmallow Dessert

2 x 150g flavoured yoghurts

1 packet marshmallows or homemade marshmallow (go to the Novelty section page 50.)

1 tin tropical fruit salad or other tinned fruit of your choice

1 bottle cream, whipped.

Combine all ingredients.

Syrup Dumplings (Instant steam puddings)

250g flour

1 egg

3 teaspoons baking powder

½ teaspoon salt

30g butter

150ml milk

Rub in dry ingredients with softened butter, add beaten egg and milk. Mix until a very soft dough. Divide into 6 balls.

Syrup: In a medium-sized pot boil 1½ cups water, ¾ cup golden syrup, 1 teaspoon lemon juice (optional). Place the dough into the boiling syrup, reduce heat and simmer for 20 minutes with lid on. NO peeking!

Serve with cream or ice-cream.

For a change, add ¼ cup shredded coconut to the syrup.

Baked Apple Delights

2 cups self-raising flour

120g butter, melted

¾ cups milk to mix.

Mix into a soft dough or pulse in a blender. Divide into six portions, spread each portion out in your hand and place a quarter of a peeled apple in it, then wrap the dough around the apple.

Place in deep baking or casserole dish, and repeat with the other portions.

Syrup: Bring to the boil 120g butter, 1 cup sugar, 1½ cups water, and 1 teaspoon vanilla essence. Pour this syrup over apple-filled dumplings.

Bake 180 degrees Celsius for 30 minutes.

Serve with cream or ice-cream.

Variations: Wrap each dough portion around either

A chocolate piece

A strawberry and a chocolate piece

A piece of crystallised ginger chopped and a quarter of a peeled pear

Or fill each portion with jam.

The list is endless.

Diabetic Pavlova

For those who are sugar-intolerant this pavlova works well.

6 egg whites

2 tablespoons cornflour

1 cup coconut

2 tablespoons Splenda or ½ teaspoon Stevia rebaudiana

Beat the egg whites until stiff, add the cornflour and beat again.

Fold in the coconut and Splenda or stevia; do not beat.

Bake at 180c for 30 minutes.

Novelty Confectionery

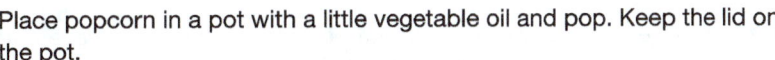

Candy Popcorn

2 cups sugar

1 cup water

½ teaspoon food colouring (optional)

Popcorn: ½ a cup makes 8 cups cooked popcorn.

Place popcorn in a pot with a little vegetable oil and pop. Keep the lid on the pot.

Into a large pot put in the sugar, water and colouring, stirring over low heat until the sugar dissolves. Boil uncovered. Test small amounts of toffee in cold water until toffee cracks. Take off the heat.

Add the cooked popcorn to the toffee, and with a wooden spoon stir the popcorn to coat it. Keep stirring the toffee and popcorn; when it cools it will separate quite quickly and become candy-coated popcorn.

Variation: Raw peanuts instead of popcorn.

Sherbert Fizz

2 tablespoons citric acid

2 tablespoons baking soda

6 tablespoons icing sugar

Flavouring: granulated drink crystals, ie Raro sachets; try to use a colour-free variety.

Sift and mix altogether, and put into small packets with a straw.

Meringues made in a microwave

Children enjoy watching the meringues rise as well as eating them with cream or ice cream.

1 egg white

350g icing sugar.

Mix the egg white with the icing sugar until it forms into a pliable dough. Roll into a log that that is the size of a two- dollar coin, then cut into 1.5 centimetre slices.

Place 6 slices in a circle on greaseproof paper in the microwave and microwave on high for 1 to 2 minutes, depending on microwave wattage. When meringue is done it should be firm to the touch; if it's still soft heat in 10-second bursts until it is firm to touch. If meringues are over-cooked they will burn very quickly and go brown inside.

Meringues keep for weeks in an air-tight container.

Lolly Cake

2 packets super wine biscuits crumbed

125g melted butter

1 tin condensed milk

Eskimos or fruit puffs.

Melt butter and add to ingredients. Place on cling wrap and make a log; wrap and place in refrigerator. Slice.

Lolly cake keeps well in the freezer to bring out for rainy days.

Home-made Chocolate

1 cup milk powder

1 cup icing sugar

3 tablespoons cocoa

250g vegetable fat (Kremelta is available at supermarkets.)

Sift dry ingredients. Melt Kremelta and add to the dry ingredients. Pour into slice tray, and cut before it hardens.

Keep in refrigerator.

Flavour combinations:

Add these to dry ingredients:

(1) Coconut (makes the chocolate very tasty)

(2) Raisins or sultanas with coconut

(3) Raisins soaked in rum

(4) Nuts and raisins

(5) Rice bubbles and coconut - add rice bubbles and coconut and place into patties to make chocolate crackle for children's parties.

(6) Or make up your own flavours.

To make white chocolate omit the cocoa and add 2 teaspoons of vanilla essence.

Home-made Marshmallow

Dissolve 2 dessertspoons of gelatine in 1 cup of boiling water. Add 2 cups sugar, vanilla and colouring (optional), beat until fluffy, pour onto toasted or plain shredded coconut or sieved icing sugar. Leave to set, and cut.

Rocky Road

To make Rocky Road combine marshmallow pieces to cooled homemade chocolate, (on page 49), then add plain or baked nuts, sultanas and coconut. Pour into a dish, place in fridge to set. Cut into portions.

Toffee Apples

225g sugar

110ml water

½ teaspoon vinegar

2 tablespoons golden syrup

25g butter

In a pot add the water and sugar, and place over a moderate heat until sugar has dissolved. Add the vinegar, golden syrup and butter. Bring to the boil and cook without stirring until it reaches the toffee stage (138C), when toffee dropped from the spoon into cold water forms into a hardened ball. This should take about 10 minutes.

Clean apples; pierce a wooden skewer into the apple. Once the toffee is ready, dip each apple into the hot toffee, turning and coating the apple.

Leave to harden on an oiled tray.

Condiments and Hints

Vegemite

250g brewers' flaked yeast (Not bread yeast or yeast granules)

2 tablespoons wheat germ

350ml soy sauce

Mix all ingredients and refrigerate.

Sweetener:

replace sugar and artificial sweeteners with Stevia rebaudiana, a natural sweetener alternative. Stevia grows well and when dried grinds to a fine powder in a coffee grinder. It is available from health food outlets. Stevia in a powder is 300 times sweeter than sugar!

Berry Jam with Stevia

500 grams each of Raspberries, Strawberries and Boysenberries.

Place in a pot with juice of 1 lemon and 1 cup of water. Bring to the boil, reduce heat and simmer until fruit has separated. Add up to 1 teaspoon or more of Stevia, then take a small amount and do a taste test. Add 50ml of glycerine, stir into jam, bottle and seal in small jars, as it does not have the keeping qualities of jam made with sugar. Refrigerate.

This is a syrupy jam and has a full intense flavour of berry fruits.

To make a thicker jam add 4 tablespoons of agar agar or gelatine when the fruit has separated. Stir in well and proceed with the stevia and glycerine.

Self-raising flour hint:

Make your own with 1 teaspoon baking powder to 1 cup plain flour.

Condensed Milk

Pour ½ cup of boiling water into a blender or a bowl to hand-beat.

Add 1 cup of milk powder

²/₃ cup sugar

3 tablespoons melted butter

½ teaspoon vanilla essence

Blend on high speed until smooth - about 30 seconds. This is the quick way.

To make a syrupy version, place ingredients in a double boiler and bring mixture to a higher heat to dissolve the milk powder.

Store in a container in the fridge.

Potato Hash Browns

3 large raw potatoes, grated

2 eggs, beaten

½ teaspoon salt

1 tablespoon milk

1 tablespoon flour

Pepper

Marjoram: fresh 1 tablespoon, chopped, or 1 teaspoon dried.

Mix all ingredients. Place large spoonfuls onto hot frypan; reduce heat to prevent burning. Cook for approximately 4 minutes a side.

Curry Powder:

2 whole small red chillies and seeds

2 tablespoons whole coriander seeds

1 tablespoon whole cumin seeds

1 teaspoon whole black peppercorns

1 teaspoon whole fenugreek seeds

½ teaspoon black mustard seeds

½ teaspoon ground ginger

½ teaspoon ground turmeric

In a dry pan roast or fry chillies, coriander, cumin, mustard seeds, peppercorns, and fenugreek over a medium heat for 2 to 3 minutes, shaking pan constantly to prevent burning. Remove from heat.

Grind the roasted spices to a powder in a mortar or coffee grinder, and then stir in the ginger and turmeric.

Mussel Marinade

This is a wonderful marinade for mussels. Steam open mussels and remove, pour marinade over them and leave to stand to absorb the marinade.

Marinade

½ cup sugar

1 cup water

1 cup spiced vinegar

Bring to boil and cool; add 1 onion, finely chopped.

Basil Pesto

1 cup packed firmly with fresh basil; use the soft stalks, too;

350ml olive oil

4 tablespoons grated parmesan

170g walnuts

3 cloves garlic

1 teaspoon salt

Put all ingredients into a blender and blend.

Place in container and refrigerate; it freezes well. Freeze into small serving-portion sizes.

Basil pesto goes well with crackers and cheese, on eggs and fish, and tossed into cooked pasta.

Sun-Dried Tomato Pesto

250g sun-dried tomatoes

20g parmesan

600ml olive oil

125g walnuts

15g garlic

80g fresh basil

2 teaspoons sugar

½ teaspoon salt

Put all ingredients into a blender and blend.

Place into containers and refrigerate.

Sun-dried tomato pesto goes well with crackers and cheese and tossed into cooked pasta.

Vinaigrette

2 garlic cloves peeled and cut in half.

Juice of ½ lemon

120ml white vinegar

Salt and ground black pepper

Pinch of sugar

500ml olive oil

3 sprigs of herbs of your choice, i.e. tarragon, basil, dill, marjoram, oregano etc.

Place all ingredients in a jar or a bottle, shake well.

Shake well again before serving.

Elderflower Champagne

This is a very enjoyable drink.

This drink can be very fizzy, so do not over-fill bottles.

4 litres water

2 1/2 cups sugar

8 heads of fresh elderflowers

2 lemons sliced

2 tablespoons white vinegar

Bring the water and sugar to the boil. Cool liquid and add the elderflower heads, sliced lemons and vinegar, and stir mixture.

Leave to sit for 24 hours, strain and bottle, and leave for 1 to 2 weeks. To bottle, re-use lemonade or Coke plastic bottles.

White Sauce

2 tablespoons of butter; melt in pot.

Add to this 1 tablespoon of flour. Cook the flour into the butter. Add milk slowly while stirring with a wooden spoon until it reaches the desired consistency. Add salt and pepper - or the seasoning mix - to taste (on page 16).

To increase or reduce the amount of sauce add more or less flour and butter.

Cheese sauces: add grated cheese when sauce is cooked.

Parsley sauces: add chopped parsley.

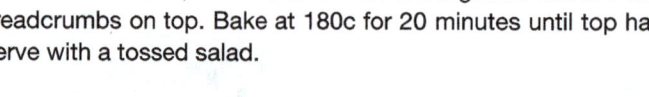

This sauce is wonderful for macaroni cheese bake.

Cook pasta to manufacturer's instructions, place pasta into an oven-proof dish, top with cheese sauce, cover sauce with extra grated cheese and sprinkle breadcrumbs on top. Bake at 180c for 20 minutes until top has crusted. Serve with a tossed salad.

Gravy Deglaze (No flour)

When the roast meat is cooked, take out of pan to rest.

The juices in the bottom of the pan makes tasty gravy.

Empty out as much fat as possible, leaving the rich juice in pan. Heat on medium heat, adding up to a cup of wine to the pan, and scraping the bottom of the pan to bring up all the flavours. Reduce juice by a quarter, add a large knob of butter to create a silky gravy, and add seasoning if required. Drizzle over roast meats.

Roux (Gravy)

Gravy is simple to make. Cook the flour in the fat from the meat, then add stock or the vegetable stock that is being used for the main meal.

First of all, take meat out of roasting pan. If there is too much fat in the pan, empty this until about three tablespoons of fat are left. Add 2 tablespoons of flour and fry the flour in the fat until the flour is a paste. Next, add the hot stock or hot water slowly to the cooked fat, stirring with a wooden spoon and picking up the meat glaze from the bottom of the pan. Keep adding the stock until a gravy consistency has been achieved. Add salt and pepper or the seasoning mix to taste (on page 16).

To increase or reduce the quantity of gravy add more or less flour and fats.

Cheese Products

Mascarpone, Crème Fraiche and Ricotta are simple and cheap to make. It will give you great pleasure to share with others that you have created these products from scratch.

Sterilize containers with 50mls of bleach added to 1 litre of water.

Mascarpone

1 litre cream

½ teaspoon tartaric acid

To make mascarpone: scald cream, cool, and add tartaric acid.

Line a sieve with damp muslin or a clean Chux cloth.

Pour mixture into sieve, place in fridge and drain overnight or until the whey has stopped dripping. Place in clean container. Mascarpone will keep for 2 weeks. Makes 500ml.

Crème Fraiche

500ml cream

250ml buttermilk or sour milk (Lemon juice added to milk to make sour milk)

Gently heat the cream and buttermilk until just below body temp, 25c. Pour the cream into a container and partly cover. Keep at this temperature for 6-8 hours or until it has thickened and tastes slightly acid.

The cream will thicken faster on a hot day. Stir and store in the refrigerator for up to 2 weeks. Makes 750ml.

Ricotta

2 litres milk

¼ cup vinegar

Salt

Place milk in a 4 litre double boiler, and add salt to taste.

Heat slowly to 85 degrees Celsius. When it has reached this temperature, stir the heated milk very, very slowly (snail's pace) while adding vinegar. Stop stirring as soon as the curd has formed.

Gently scoop out the curd into a lined colander and allow it to cool, then place it in a clean container. Ricotta can be used immediately; otherwise store it in the refrigerator.

Cottage Cheese

1 litre milk

2 teaspoons rennet

Heat milk to lukewarm and remove from heat. Add rennet, stir slowly for thirty seconds, and allow to set.

Break up the curd and put it into a sieve lined with muslin or a Chux cloth. Stand overnight to separate the curds and whey. Place in a clean container; it can be used immediately or stored in the refrigerator.

Sour Cream (1)

1 cup cream

1 tablespoon buttermilk

Recipe can be increased: just keep doubling ingredients.

In a double boiler bring cream up to bubble-froth stage. Cool to room temperature, in a cold water bath in the sink.

Add buttermilk, cover and let stand for 24 to 48 hours.

Stir and place into clean container and refrigerate. This will keep for up to 3 to 4 weeks.

Sour Cream (2)

1 cup cream

¼ cup of original sour cream culture or buttermilk

Put all ingredients into a screw-top jar and stand at room temperature for 24 hours until thick.

Refrigerate.

Note: Buttermilk is a by-product of butter-making. It freezes and can be used for cooking - but not drinking! - when frozen.

Rennet

Liquid vegetarian rennet can be made from stinging nettle or whole dandelion plant and flowers. Put a large bunch in a pot, cover and bring to boil. Leave to cool for 2 hours and use a tablespoon of the liquid.

Rennet also comes from the white sap of figs, lemon juice, white vinegar, citric acid. These can all be used in cheese-making, though they will not make a hard cheese. For that, you'll need commercial rennet.

Yoghurt

1 litre milk; any kind

3 Tablespoons non-fat dried milk powder (optional)

Starter: 2 tablespoons existing yogurt with live cultures,

i.e. natural yogurt or acidophilus yogurt.

Whisk milk powder into a little of the milk until completely dissolved; this will help thicken the yoghurt more easily and add more nutrition. Then add rest of milk, and stir.

Heat the milk until it starts to froth or the temperature reaches 85C. Do not boil or burn the milk. Microwaving is good: it takes 8 to 10 minutes on high, depending on the microwave wattage.

Cool the milk to room temperature or baby-milk temperature. Add the starter yoghurt to the cooled milk.

Keep the yoghurt warm in either a yoghurt maker or an Easy-Yo container. Or you could use an oven where the temperature is maintained at 38C (having the oven light on might be enough); or in a double boiler - or maybe put it in your car on a sunny day. Just use your common sense and a thermometer.

After 8 hours the yoghurt should have a thickish appearance, and the whey - a thin yellow liquid - will form on top. You can pour off the whey or stir into yoghurt.

Refrigerated, this yoghurt will keep for 1 to 2 weeks.

Use 2 tablespoons of this yoghurt to create the next yoghurt within 5 days to keep the bacteria growing.

Yoghurt Cream Cheese

1kg plain yoghurt

Put yoghurt in a sieve lined with muslin or a Chux cloth, place over a bowl, and leave in the fridge for about 1 to 2 days to drain. Once drained place in clean containers.

The drained liquid is called whey and the solid part is called curds. Have the curds as plain cream cheese, or add herbs, spices, jams, fresh fruit and nuts to create a tasty cheese spread.

Whey is full of amazing enzymes: add it to your soup, pikelets, pancakes, and muffins.

Yoghurt Iceblocks

Place yoghurt into small plastic cup containers or iceblock containers. Pureed fruit or chopped fruit can be added to the yogurt to make fruit-filled yogurt blocks.

To centre the all-important popsicle stick, place tin foil over container and poke popsicle stick through the middle. Freeze.

Sour Cream Dip

1 cup or 250g sour cream

Salt and pepper to taste.

Chopped herbs of your choice: chives, coriander, tarragon, dill, spring onions: you may want to add calendula petals for character.

Cottage Cheese and Tuna Spread

1 cup cottage cheese

1 tin tuna, drained

2 medium or 1 large stalk of chopped celery

2 tablespoons mayonnaise

Mix all together and use as a filling for sandwiches.

Roll it in fresh sandwich bread as an alternative to asparagus rolls.

Or use it as a dip, or as a potato alternative.

Ricotta Terrine

1kg ricotta

3 eggs, beaten

3 tablespoons chopped herbs (make a mixture from the following: chives, marjoram, oregano, tarragon, parsley, salad burnet).

Place ricotta in a bowl and beat until smooth, add the beaten eggs and mix into ricotta. Add the chopped herbs and fold into the mixture.

Place into a terrine or a loaf tin, and stand this tin in a basin of water.

Bake for 30 – 40 minutes at 180c

Place on a platter drizzled with olive oil sprinkled either with paprika or chopped herbs and serve with a salad and ciabatta bread.

Avocado Dip

2 ripe avocados

2 tablespoons lemon juice

1 garlic clove, minced

2 tablespoons finely chopped onion

½ cup of chopped coriander leaves

2 tablespoons chopped red chilli

1 tomato with seeds removed, chopped finely.

Salt and pepper to taste

Scoop out the flesh from the avocados and mash. Add all remaining ingredients, and mix well.

Serve with rice crackers, corn chips or vegetable sticks.

Medicinal

If any condition persists you should seek further advice from a health professional.

There are many herbal remedies - too numerous to be covered by this book, in which I have picked common herbs and weeds that are in a lot of our gardens.

These are common weeds that can be used as an everyday alternative to pharmaceutical medicines and a natural alternative.

Cleaver (Galium aparine)

Cleaver is a tonic for the lymphatic system, as it strengthens lymphatic circulation. It has anti-inflammatory and anti-cancer properties.

It is used to treat urinary, cystitis and ulcer problems as well as glandular fever, tonsillitis, chronic fatigue, hepatitis. It's effective, taken externally and internally, for eczema and psoriasis. It is a powerful diuretic. It is very high in silica. And as an infusion it is helpful for insomnia.

Gather a bundle of cleavers, put into a large jug, fill with cold water and let it sit overnight. Drink it the next day; the taste is not unlike cucumber.

As a tincture, use 2 to 3mls three times a day.

If you didn't know its name, cleaver is that persistent sticky weed that attaches its leaves and seeds to our animals and clothing.

Chickweed (Stellaria Media)

Chickweed grows everywhere and is packed full of nutrition: it contains vitamins A,B,B1,B2,B12,C,D and minerals copper, iron, calcium, sodium, potassium, silica, manganese, phosphorus and zinc. WOW! Why would you ever weed this plant?

It can be taken internally for rheumatism and chest infections, and externally for itchy skin conditions like eczema, psoriasis, and vaginitis, as well as for ulcers, boils and abscesses.

It can be taken as an infusion: drink up to 3 cups per day.

Or put chickweed into a juicer, eat it raw in salads or in a Vegemite sandwich, as a green folded into an omelette, or blanched and used as a hot green vegetable.

It can also be made into an ointment, poultice, and tincture or oil infusion.

Amazing! And this is a persistent weed that is in our very own garden!

Dandelion (Taraxacum Officinale)

This bitter compound stimulates appetite and promotes digestion, it stimulates the liver and gallbladder, and it is blood-cleansing. It also helps with nausea and morning sickness.

It is an excellent source of vitamin A, having five times more than carrot. And it contains calcium, sodium, potassium, selenium, zinc, silicic acid, copper, iron and sulphur and antioxidants.

Take it in leaf form either from a juicer or in a salad; or as a tincture (4 to 10mls daily).

An infusion of flowers and leaves taken in a dosage of 10 to 20mls three times a day can help with headaches, menstrual cramps or as a cardiac tonic.

Plantain (Plantago Lanceolata, Rib Wort and Plantago Major, Greater Plantain)

My favourite weed is plantain (Plantago). Squeezed plantain is very effective on insect bites and bee and wasp stings, and on cuts it is a natural antiseptic. Squeeze it in your fingers until the juice comes through, and apply to insect bites. It instantly brings relief to that itch. Reapply it if itch is persistent.

Medicinally, plantain is taken internally for diarrhoea, haemorrhoids, cystitis, bronchitis, sinusitis, asthma, hay fever, and gastric ulcers; and for wounds, bruises, insect bites, ulcers, and shingles. It even works as an eye wash.

It's taken as a tincture (1 to 4mls 3 times daily), and it can also be made into an oil infusion or ointment.

Remarkable! And this grows in our very own lawn!

Sage (Salvia Officinalis)

Cleanses the respiratory and digestive tracts of mucus, normalizing the central nervous system, and reducing fevers, helping with night sweats, and soothing sore throats.

Sage contains oestrogen which helps with female problems.

This is a safe cough suppressant and expectorant, even for children. Drink it as a tea.

Stinging Nettle (Urtica Dioica)

Is very rich in chlorophyll, iron, lime, potassium, phosphorus and sulphur and contains vitamins A, B and C.

A tea of stinging nettle helps lymphatic ailments, dropsy, gallstones and kidney stones, and is a blood purifier.

Boil the leaves and drink as a tea for an infusion for anaemia sufferers, gout, arthritis and kidney disorders and stones, obesity and sciatica.

During pollen season drink nettle tea 3 times a day to relieve hay fever.

Yarrow (Achillea Millefolium)

Contains bitter compounds tannins, phosphorus, asparagines, nitrates, proteins, acetic acid and malic acid.

Yarrow is antispasmodic, antiseptic, blood cleansing and stimulating. It's a coagulant to stop bleeding, and a tonic, helpful with colds and fevers.

Yarrow helps relieve menstrual cramps and pelvic tension, it helps with hormone balance in puberty and menopause, and it strengthens blood vessels, varicose veins and haemorrhoids.

It can also help relax tight muscles and spasms.

Take it as an infusion 3 times a day or, if feverish, 1 hourly.

As a tincture the dose is 2 to 4mls three times a day.

For a more palatable drink add lemon balm.

Thyme (Thymus)

When an individual comes into my household with a cold I burn essential oil of thyme and spray-mist the rooms, or I put a pot on the stove with water and a large bunch of thyme and let it simmer to let all the air become infused with thyme.

Phenol, a common commercial disinfectant, has a germ-killing rating of 1. Thyme on the other hand is 12.2! One has to ask where and why did we stop trusting these herbs that have been used safely for hundreds of years?

Other herbs that have a high count of phenol are lavender, rosemary, rue, rose, cinnamon and cloves.

Thyme consists of vitamins A and C, niacin and thiamine, and minerals calcium, chromium, cobalt, iron, magnesium, phosphorus, potassium, selenium, silicon, sodium, tin and zinc.

Thyme soothes coughs and as an expectorant eases asthma and respiratory complaints. It is a calmative and eases wind. Thyme lowers fevers.

*(**Caution:** do not use essential oil of thyme if pregnant as it is a uterine stimulant.)*

Make it into an infusion for sore throats: gargle and then swallow. Sip as tea or as an infusion for headaches, and as a tincture or infusion for respiratory infections.

Definition of first aid terms

Poultice: Involves the application of fresh plant foliage crushed and placed direct onto the skin.

For example, apply crushed yarrow direct to a cut to stop the flow of blood: yarrow is a natural blood coagulant. Or apply crushed plantain to insect bites, or take a split leaf from the aloe vera and apply the gel direct to a burn; the gel is cooling and healing and takes away the pain and sting from burns and sunburn. Reapply as necessary until the pain has been alleviated.

Compresses: Are poultices applied with heat. Place herbs into a fabric or muslin bag and wet the compress in boiling water. When it has cooled to the touch apply to the affected area.

Tea: This is made by pouring boiling water over fresh or dried herbs to extract and release the volatile oils in the herbs.

The liquid is strained and sipped. Or you can place herbs in a coffee plunger pot for ease of use. Drink 3 cups a day, or more for chronic ailments.

Infusion: Is the same as a tea but made in larger quantities and from a larger amount of herbs. This is a stronger brew and can be reheated. An infusion dose for an adult is two cups a day.

The term is "The bitterer the better", i.e. when the volatile oils are infused to a strong decoction they're more effective – though not as nice for the consumer!

Tincture: Fresh or dried herbs in alcohol (I normally use vodka). This lasts forever. Pack tight a jar with fresh chopped herbs or dried herbs, fill the jar with alcohol and leave in a cool dark place for six weeks, then strain, bottle, label and date.

Suggested general tincture dosage: 1 teaspoon to 50kg of body weight three times a day.

Oil infusion: Gather a large bunch of fresh herbs. Finely chop and tightly pack into a clean jar, fill with olive oil, then run a knife down the sides to release the air. Place jar in a dish so that oil can leach out, then seal and leave in a cool dark place for 6 weeks. Strain through a sieve and bottle, label and date.

Ointments: Melt 28g of beeswax in a double boiler.

Gently heat 250mls of infused oil until hot enough to touch and stir into the melted beeswax.

Pour into clean jars and label. Adding more or less beeswax or infused oil will make a softer or harder ointment.

camomile

Suggested First Aid

Caution:

1. Some herbs could interact negatively with medication prescribed for you. Always seek advice.

2. If the condition persists you should seek further advice from a health care professional.

Acne: Rinse the skin with an infusion of chamomile which is purifying. Yarrow infusion helps eliminate toxins. Catnip, lavender and thyme infusions are antiseptic.

Asthma: Stinging nettle is an expectorant. Made as a tea it is excellent for any mucous problems such as asthma, bronchitis, and colds.

A sage infusion cleans the respiratory and digestive tracts of mucus, normalizes the nervous system and improves memory.

Arthritis: Aloe Vera: split a leaf and take up to 2 tablespoons of the gel 2 to 3 times a day to relive joint pain. Make up an infusion of chamomile, dandelion, garlic, meadowsweet, parsley and nettle.

Meadowsweet contains salicylate, the active ingredient in aspirin. Salicylate is commonly associated with willow, but few people know that salicylates were originally obtained from meadowsweet, not willow.

Burns: Try fresh aloe vera gel from a cut leaf - a must in every kitchen. Place on burn and hold for a short time; replace if burn still stings. Or:

Freshly-grated ginger (apply direct to burn);

Calendula leaf and flower infusion (bathe burn);

Plantago major or Plantago lanceolate infusion (bathe burn).

Broken bones: Comfrey, which is also known as knitbone. Comfrey contains a substance called allantoin, which is a cell proliferent, known for its healing properties for broken bones. Comfrey has a remarkable effect on persistent ulcers, too: pulverize the leaf and place on the ulcer.

Bruising: Comfrey leaf: dip it in hot water and apply directly.

Wormwood or chamomile poultice: apply direct to bruise.

Calendula flowers and leaf: applied in infusion, oil or ointment form.

Equal parts cider vinegar and cold water: soak a clean cloth and hold on the bruise for at least an hour.

Blisters: Crushed plantain or dock leaf: apply as poultice.

Crushed chickweed or calendula petals: Make into a tea and bathe blister.

Coughs: Tea of plantain, sage, thyme or comfrey.

Tincture of plantain.

10ml apple cider vinegar and 2 teaspoons honey in a glass: sip throughout the day.

Colic: Dill water: infuse 13g bruised dill seeds in 1 cup boiling water, strain. Dosage: babies 5mls three times a day.

Caraway seeds: infused as for dill water.

Catnip: infused or as a tea.

Colds: Echinacea: any sign of a cold, or even if you have merely been in contact with someone with a cold, take echinacea straight away. It immediately boosts your immune system.

Tea of yarrow, peppermint, catnip or elder-flower; or:

In a cup put a pinch of cayenne pepper, large pinch of ginger or slice of fresh ginger, juice of a lemon, and honey. Pour in boiling water and drink.

(Cayenne strengthens and stimulates the circulatory and digestive system.)

Constipation: Psyllium seeds and husks, figs, licorice, stewed rhubarb or flaxseeds.

Cuts: Squeezed Plantain, yarrow leaves or calendula petals applied directly to the cut. Alternatively, these can be made into a tea and applied to bathe the cut.

Cider vinegar and water: apply in equal parts.

Deodorant: White or herbal vinegar of your choice: wipe on your underarms. This neutralizes odour; it does not stop perspiration.

Lovage: make into a tea and wipe underarms.

Recipe for a natural deodorant under Natural Body Products (page 90)

Depression: Meditation rebalances the chakra points; take time to focus on the inner spirit.

St John's Wort evens out the lows of mild depression.

Diarrhoea: One teaspoon cider vinegar in a glass of water six times a day.

Plantain boiled in milk. Comfrey, meadowsweet, catnip or self-heal tea. Unripe or green apples, stewed.

Digestive Tracts: Aloe Vera: split a leaf and take up to 2 tablespoons of the gel 2 to 3 times a day to relive bloat and irritable bowel syndrome.

Drug Addiction: Feverfew and Skullcap administered as a tonic can help with symptoms of narcotic, alcohol and tranquillizer withdrawal.

Make a tea or infusion, and drink 3 times a day to help withdrawal symptoms.

Eyes: Tea of self-heal or chickweed eye wash for conjunctivitis and sties, and tired, itchy or strained eyes.

For sties, place baby shampoo on a cotton wool bud and wipe sty gently to clean the blocked pore three times a day.

Eye Wash: Rock salt: 1 teaspoon dissolved in 500ml of boiling water, leave to cool to room temperature.

Eczema: Chickweed, cleavers or calendula: poultice or oil infusion.

Chervil: poultice.

Fevers: Tea of Ginger and cayenne, thyme, yarrow, elder flower or sage.

Bathe baby's feet in cider vinegar.

Fluid Retention: Celery: eat the stalks; or cleaver tea. These are both very diuretic.

Foot Odour: Wipe or bathe feet with a solution of one part cider vinegar to one part warm water.

Baking soda: sprinkle in shoes. (Try adding essential oil to the baking soda.)

Gout: Comfrey, bay, chicory, couch grass or dandelion: as an infusion.

Cucumber helps eliminate the uric acid that accumulates with sufferers of rheumatism and gout.

Haemorrhoids: Dilute vinegar and apply to haemorrhoids to soothe itching and burning.

Feverfew: apply externally, as a poultice.

Hair: Vinegar has many wonderful uses on your hair, it is a colour preserver, conditioner, frizz reducer; it can fight dandruff, help with head lice. It gives your hair extra shine; rinse with it to neutralize shampoo and product build-up.

Chamomile tea applied as a conditioner to blond hair will bring out the blond shine.

Sage and rosemary can darken hair.

Sage and yarrow can darken grey hair and add lustre.

Calendula flowers or henna can redden hair.

Try elderberries for black hair.

Hair loss: Stinging nettle is a scalp stimulant. Make an infusion of 1 cup grated root and leaf in a litre of water and apply to the scalp as a conditioner. Alternatively, dampen a cloth with the infusion and leave on the scalp for half an hour. Apply often.

Head Lice Essential Oils: Combine essential oils of 25 drops rosemary oil, 25 drops lavender oil, 13 drops geranium oil

12 drops eucalyptus oil, 10 drops tea tree oil and 75 ml vegetable oil or neem oil. Saturate the hair and ensure it is all covered, then wrap it in plastic cling wrap or a shower cap and leave for 2 hours.

Add shampoo and rub in well, rinsing thoroughly and combing through with a nit comb. Repeat 3 days later. This leaves the hair lustrous and shining.

Headaches: Tea of lemon balm, catnip, rosemary, mint, chamomile flowers or feverfew leaves.

Lavender essential oil massaged into the temples.

Violet or willow infusion or tea. (Violet and willow contain salicylates like aspirin.)

Hay Fever: Stinging nettle tea: take before and during the pollen season. Nettle is a blood tonic and purifier.

Chamomile: Inhale the vapour and drink it as a tea.

Heartburn: Cider vinegar: one teaspoon in a glass of warm water prior to eating.

Lemon balm tea, dill, licorice, peppermint or ginger tea: drink prior to eating

High Blood Pressure and High Cholesterol: Take garlic either as cloves or in tablet form: to avoid bad breath, chew and swallow parsley to neutralize the garlic. Or place a garlic clove in your sock: it is then absorbed through the skin, although the garlic smell also carries through the skin pores.

Hot Flushes: One to two teaspoons of cider vinegar in a glass of cold water three times a day.

Tea of sage or hyssop.

Indigestion: Mix ½ teaspoon baking soda in ½ glass of warm water and drink.

Catnip, lemon balm, thyme, savory, oregano, fennel, dandelion, coriander, caraway, bay or ginger: any of these as a tea can alleviate discomfort.

Insect Bites: Plantain: squeeze in fingers until the juice comes through; apply to bites. Reapply if itch is persistent.

Parsley, dock, chickweed, calendula, penny royal, dock or comfrey: squeeze or crush and apply to sting.

Dandelion: apply the white sap direct.
Essential oil of lavender: apply direct.

Insect Repellent: Almond oil, grape seed oil or rice bran oil: add two drops of essential oils (eucalyptus, cloves, peppermint, rosemary or citronella) and rub onto your skin.

Feverfew, wormwood, elder or chamomile leaves and flowers: make an infusion and apply to the skin.

Insomnia: Dried hop flowers and lavender flower heads: take 3 to 4 handfuls of each, place in a small pillow bag, and place into your pillow case or under your pillow. This herbal pillow should calm the nerves and help you sleep.

Passion flower, hawthorn berries or flowers, dandelion, chamomile, catnip, valerian: heat an infusion of one or more of these herbs in milk, let it stand for 5 minutes, strain and drink. You may want to dissolve about 6 cubes of dark chocolate into the milk for a hot chocolate drink.

Liver: Dandelion: 2 leaves a day keeps your liver at bay.

Dandelion leaves or milk thistle: as a tea.

Asparagus: eat steamed or raw.

Lemon juice: first thing in the morning to stimulate the bile flow in the gallbladder and liver.

Olive oil: combine with lemon juice for gallstones.

Makeup Removal: Sesame oil or baby oil.

Memory: Gingko: take as an herbal tea drink three times a day for two weeks, to increase memory and improve blood circulation to the brain. Taken this way before an exam may have a good effect on the memory.

Motion and Morning Sickness: Ginger, lemon balm, or savory: sip as an infusion to alleviate nausea.

Nappy Rash: Try sesame oil to treat nappy rash. Also: dry cornflour powder, applied direct to skin instead of baby powder.

Pimples: Dandelion: use the white sap.

Cider vinegar: dab direct onto pimple.

Honey: apply direct.

Oil of plantain or chickweed: apply as a poultice.

Meadow sweet or valerian: Make a tea and apply to skin eruptions.

Prostate: Saw palmetto is effective in reducing and returning the prostrate to normal. Also helps with impotence in most men.

Radiation Treatment: To relive radiation treatments split an aloe vera leaf and take up to 2 tablespoons of the gel 2 to 3 times a day prior to and after radiation treatment. Aloe vera is soothing on the digestive tract and can alleviate nausea while going through treatment.

During radiation treatment place an ice pack on top of head to stop burning pain.

Rheumatism: Cucumber helps eliminate uric acid that accumulates with sufferers of rheumatism and gout.

Sea-Sickness: Ginger: Sip an infusion to alleviate nausea, or use the suggestions for motion sickness.

Skin: Vinegar: apply diluted as a face toner; it revitalizes and helps to keep skin blemishes reduced.

Sunburn: Aloe vera: split a leaf in half and apply onto sunburn. Leave gel to dry; reapply at intervals.

Vinegar: spray on direct to burn to soothe area.

Sesame oil: protects the skin from sunburn by screening out ultraviolet rays.

Sore Throat: Sage: gargle and swallow tincture.

Tea of sage, thyme or self-heal.

Cider vinegar: mix of 1 tablespoon and a glass of warm water. Gargle every hour and swallow.

Stomach Ulcers: Aloe Vera: split a leaf and take up to 2 tablespoons of the gel 2 to 3 times a day to relieve stomach ulcers.

Chickweed, licorice, sage or plantain: as an infusion.

Olive oil: for peptic ulcers.

Stinging Nettle Sting: Dock, plantain or chickweed: crush and apply direct to sting.

Toothache: chew on a sage leaf, plantain leaf or clove.

Oil of cloves: rub on the area.

Cider vinegar: apply direct to the area.

These will help to alleviate the pain until you see the dentist.

Tooth Cleaner: rub a sage leaf on your teeth; very refreshing.

Thrush or Vaginal Irritation: Oral thrush: use acidophilus yoghurt or rinse mouth with sesame oil or a tea of thyme.

Vaginal thrush: a few tablespoons of cider vinegar in bath water and apply to vaginal area.

Sesame oil: apply direct to vaginal area.

Urinary: Cranberry juice or tablets protect against urinary infections and formation of stones; they acidify and deodorise the urine.

Vomit Smells: Sprinkle the area and clothing with baking soda to take away odour.

Warts: Dandelion: apply the white sap direct to warts twice daily.

Figs: use the white sap as for dandelion.

Vinegar: apply to a plaster and place on the wart; replace daily for a week.

Worms: Onion and garlic tea.

Raw carrots and pumpkin seeds: eat before breakfast.

Wellbeing and Wellness: Hormones control our body. They affect our state of mind.

The major glands are the Pituitary, Pineal, Thyroid, Thymus, Adrenal, Pancreas Ovary and Testis.

These energy centres are called the chakras, a word which comes from the Sanskrit (Hindu) word meaning wheel or disc.

Chakras are our energy centres. They are the openings for life and energy to flow into and out of our aura. Their function is to vitalize the physical body and to bring about the development of our self-consciousness. They are associated with our physical, mental and emotional interactions.

Many people of today tend to live inside their head. Their whole world is governed by thoughts and many of those thoughts become fears and anxieties: worries about not having enough material goods, or what others think; fears of losing a loved one, or losing themselves. As these patterns are repeated the mind becomes accustomed to them and cannot let go.

Take time to walk out in nature to rebalance, and meditate to reactivate your energy points and bring peace to your mind.

When we are centred or balanced with self, new doors open.

Then we are open to a greater consciousness of the self, our soul, our journey.

Herbal Cosmetics

Masks

Masks are placed direct onto the face and left for 20 minutes.

Make up your own combination from the list below, according to your skin type.

Test for allergy reaction on a small area of skin for two days. If there is any reaction try another combination and redo the allergy test.

Masks cleanse, nourish and stimulate the skin. Masks will often clear up blemishes.

Honey is a healer and a moisturizer, and helps in clearing blemishes.

Citrus fruits area all-natural toners and astringents.

Grapes, apples and pears are nourishing and moisturizing.

Strawberries, cucumber, pumpkin and marrow reduce oiliness.

Melons, tangerines, apricots and peaches refine coarse skin.

Oatmeal (not instant) or almonds, ground-up and made into a paste with milk, soften, smooth and add oils to the skin.

Buttermilk, yoghurt and egg white dry and tighten the skin.

Fruit Mask

Here's a natural fruit peel made with Kiwifruit and papaya.

Peel and chop half a kiwifruit, and sieve the fruit into a bowl.

Add the juice of two squeezed limes.

Sieve half a papaya into another bowl, and place this over a double boiler. (This is a pot with boiling water in the bottom, with a bowl that rests on the lip of the pot so that the hot water is around the bottom of the pot. Also known as a bain marie)

Add 1 tablespoon of vegetable gelatine, carrageen or agar to the papaya, heat and whisk until the mixture thickens and becomes glutinous, add the kiwifruit and mix.

Apply to the face and leave for between 10 minutes and 1 hour and wash off.

This mask keeps in the fridge for 2 days.

Note: Allergy-test a small skin area first; if any irritation occurs wash off.

Parsley Mask

This mask reduces oiliness and helps clear the skin of blackheads.

Make a strong infusion of parsley and apply some of the liquid, mixed with buttermilk or honey to make spreadable, over the skin.

Leave for 20 minutes.

Parsley

Skin Cleansers

Herb Milk Cleanser

Chop a half cup of herbs, either sage, violets, chamomile, lavender, comfrey or rosemary. Pour over a cup of milk and leave for four hours, then strain and use the milk as a cleanser.

Oily Skin or Face Make-up Remover

Powdered milk made into a paste of milky consistency. Rub over face with cotton wool and rinse clean.

Toners and Astringents

(1) Herbal vinegars diluted with water and dabbed on with cotton wool.

(2) Rose, lavender or elderberry flowers, sage leaves or blackberry leaves: place herbs into a cup, pour over boiling water and leave for 2 hours. To use, strain and apply with cotton-wool balls.

Moisturiser

There are many ways of making moisturisers.

Beeswax and rose water can be purchased at some health food outlets and chemists.

84ml Olive oil

28g Beeswax

28g Rose water

In a double boiler put the oil and wax and heat until wax melts. Mix in rose water. Add more rose water for a lighter cream, or use less beeswax.

Stir until it cools.

Stevia

Toothpaste

This toothpaste avoids many of the artificial ingredients that are added to commercial toothpastes.

3 teaspoons baking soda

1 teaspoon salt

1 teaspoon glycerine (supermarkets stock glycerine)

Few drops of peppermint essential oil, or small quantity cinnamon or cloves; or a combination of all.

To sweeten - but not essential - add Stevia rebaudiana (from health food shops)

Add water to make a paste. The glycerine is a sweetener.

Store at room temperature, in a container where it won't dry out and it is able to be squeezed onto a tooth brush.

Herbal Body Scrub

Skin of two lemons

50g each of peppermint or mint, rosemary, eucalyptus leaves

2 tablespoons ground black pepper.

Place all in a pot and add 300mls of olive oil. Heat through and simmer for 2 minutes, the strain in a sieve lined with a cloth.

400g sea salts: add enough of the strained oil to form a paste. Pour into a jar. Top up with the rest of the oil, and garnish with ground black pepper, lemon zest and eucalyptus leaf.

Use as a body scrub.

Deodorant

This natural deodorant is fun to make and avoids the chemicals that are added to commercial deodorants.

Pine resin: from health food outlets. (Or you can harvest your own: in a pine forest look for cut or damaged trunks. From these scars the pine produces a resin that looks like dried glue. Gather this when it's dry.) The resin is a potent antiseptic, anti-fungal and anti-bacterial.

Gather a bunch of pine needles to make a tincture.

Tincture: In a large jar place finely chopped pine needles, bay leaves, thyme and the peel of 1 lemon and 1 orange.

Pour vodka over chopped herbs to cover. Leave in a cool place for 2 to 6 weeks to infuse.

Crush and grind half a teaspoon of resin in a pestle to a fine powder. Add a tablespoon of vodka to mix and dissolve the resin.

To make up deodorant: add 3 tablespoons of tincture with the dissolved resin to a 100mls of orange blossom water or rose petal water.

Place in a pump spray bottle.

Household Cleaning Alternative

There are safe alternative cleaners that are chemical free and can have a positive effect upon your health.

Phenol, a common commercial disinfectant, has a germ-killing rating of 1, while thyme's is 12.2! One has to ask where and why did we stop using these herbs that have worked safely for hundreds of years?

Other herbs that have a high count of phenol are lavender, rosemary, rue, rose, cinnamon and cloves.

Baking Soda: (Sodium Bicarbonate) it cleans and deodorises and is environmentally friendly. It is slightly alkaline and cuts through grease and dirt.

Use baking soda in the kitchen and bathroom as a scourer; apply direct to a damp cloth. To make an even more powerful cleaner add vinegar.

Borax: Is a natural mineral and is water-soluble. Borax has many uses in the laundry: it cleans, disinfects and is a water softener.

Helps to stop mildew and mould, and removes stains.

Borax is available from commercial cleaners, soap-makers and fertilizer outlets.

Salt: Absorbs oils. As a scourer, it kills bacteria through a dehydrating action, and is a mild antiseptic.

Salt added to boiling water makes a natural saline solution for mouth and eye washes.

Washing Soda: Is a water softener and grease-cutter.

Place a handful in a bucket of hot water for cleaning walls and floors.

Helps rid pet houses and bird cages of lice.

Important: Make certain you only use washing soda on surfaces such as glass and stone, as this amount specified above can peel off paint and wax. Will remove scum off glass shower doors, but do not put on fibrous walls. Use gloves; it can irritate the skin.

Vinegar: has been used for many centuries, but sadly in our commercially-saturated world the value of this versatile product has been forgotten. Vinegar is anti-bacterial: vinegar was one of the main factors that counteracted the Black Plague in Europe.

Recipes for Household Cleaning Alternatives

Baby-Bottle Cleaner: Soak baby bottles in baking soda and water; rinse well before use.

Blocked Drains: Pour a handful of baking soda down the drain followed by a cupful of vinegar. Leave for a few minutes then flush with water.

Bloodstains: Mix vinegar and baking soda to a paste, place on stain and leave overnight.

Cleaners for Copper, Chrome, Silver & Stainless Steel:

Copper: lemon juice and salt made into a paste.

Chrome: wipe with vinegar and shine with baby oil.

Silver: bring to the boil 2 litres of water with 1 teaspoon of baking soda, 1 teaspoon of salt and a piece of aluminium foil. Place silverware in the solution and boil for 3 minutes.

Stainless steel: Baking soda and water made into a paste.

Dishwasher Alternative: Make a mixture of 2 tablespoons of baking soda and 2 tablespoons of borax; use this for each wash load.

Glass Cleaner: For smear-free glass add vinegar to water and clean windows, wiping clean with a scrunched-up newspaper.

Glue and Sticky Labels: Eucalyptus oil releases the sticky glue left behind by labels.

Kitchen and Bathroom Cleaner: To 1 cup of baking soda, add a few drops of essential oils. Mix well and leave until the oils have fully penetrated. Use as a scourer with a damp cloth.

Kitchen essential oils suggestion: Citrus, Thyme, Rosemary or Cinnamon.

Bathroom essential oil suggestion: Clove, Lavender, Cinnamon, Peppermint, Eucalyptus, Pine or Lemon.

Rust Stains: Make a paste of lemon juice and salt and place on rust stains; leave to work for a few hours.

Spot Stain Removal: Mix in a bottle ¼ cup dishwashing liquid

¼ cup glycerine and 1½ cups water. Use a little on each stain.

Smelly Fridge: Place an open container of baking soda in a fridge. It will absorb the food odours; change it frequently.

Tar: Eucalyptus oil helps with the removal of tar.

Room Deodorizer 1: Fill a 120ml spray bottle with cooled boiled water and add 20 drops of essential oil. Spray-mist the room.

Herb suggestions for Room Deodorizer: lavender, lemon verbena, rosemary, lemon balm, rose petals.

Room Deodorizer 2: Fill a spray bottle with herbal vinegar and spray-mist the room. To make herbal vinegar, follow instructions below.

Herbal Vinegar: Fill a jar with fresh herbs (suggestions: basil, bay, dill, lemon balm, marjoram, mint, rosemary, tarragon, thyme). Fill with white vinegar, seal jar and put into a dark cool place for 4 to 6 weeks to infuse. Strain bottle and label. It is now ready to use.

Fabric Softener and Deodorizer: Add 5 drops of essential oil (optional) to a litre of white vinegar. Add 1 to 2 cups to the final rinse water. This can help sensitive-skin sufferers.

Ballpoint pen marks: White vinegar: dab full strength on mark using a cloth or sponge. Repeat until the mark is gone.

Chicken Coop: To keep bird-lice at bay plant wormwood (Artemisia) around the chicken house.

Clean coop with washing soda.

Cockroaches: Make a mixture of borax and sugar to get rid of cockroaches.

Dog Runs: Place pennyroyal mint under your pet's bedding to keep fleas at bay. Rub pennyroyal mint on their coat as a flea deterrent.

Dog Flea Bath: Add vinegar and baking soda to bath water. This will deter fleas and leave your dog with a shiny soft coat.

Insect Repellent: Stop ants and other insects invading your home. Pour full-strength vinegar or lemon juice around tracking area, or sprinkle cayenne pepper or thyme essential oil at entry point.

Sand Pit: Pour full-strength white vinegar around children's sand pit to stop cats using it as a litter box. Reapply every two months.

Herbal Salt Scourer: In an ice cream container add a 2cm layer of salt then a layer of herbs (suggested: lavender, thyme, and rose). Continue to alternate salt and herbs. Cover and leave for between a week and a month. Sieve out herbs.

Use salt as a scourer, cleanser and degreaser when cleaning benches, basins and baths.

In the Pantry: Bay leaves in jars of rice, flour, cereals and pulses will deter weevils and moths.

Bay leaves

Herbal Carpet Deodorizer:

2 cups baking soda

4 teaspoons ground cinnamon

4 teaspoons ground cloves

4 tablespoons dried rosemary

4 tablespoons dried thyme

4 tablespoons dried sage

4 tablespoons dried mint

4 tablespoons dried lavender

4 tablespoons dried pennyroyal mint (flea deterrent)

A few drops of your favourite essential oil (optional).

Blend the herbs in a blender; add the baking soda and mix.

Use a jar with a sealed lid to infuse. Have another lid with nail holes punched in the lid to use as the sprinkler.

Sprinkle onto carpet and leave for 30 minutes and vacuum. Re-seal and use anytime. Do not use on wet carpet.

Make up your own herbal combinations - have fun!

Lavender

Plants that purify the air

Common poisons that are found in our environment are

Formaldehyde, Benzene and Trichloroethylene.
These are some plants that absorb dangerous chemicals through the whole plant and are very useful to have around the home.

Spider Plant (Chlorophytum elatum).

Azaleas (Rhododendron indicum)

Mother-in-Law's Tongue (Sanseveria laurentii)

Poinsettias (Euphorbia pulcherrina)

Heart Leaf (Philodendron indicum)

Fig Trees (Ficus moraceae)
are all effective in removing formaldehyde

English Ivy (Hedera helix)

Marginata (Dracaena marginata)
are effective in removing Benzene.

Peace Lily (Spathiphyllum)

Dragon Tree (Dracaena deremensis)
are effective at removing trichloroethylene.

Peace Lily

In the Garden

Vegetable garden spray 1: Crush 3 cloves garlic, 1 onion, 1 teaspoon chilli powder and mix with 2 teaspoons paraffin oil, 1 litre of water. Allow to stand for 24 hours; strain and bottle. Use 1 teaspoon to a ½ litre of water.

Vegetable garden spray 2: Make up a solution of a teaspoon of laundry detergent in a half bucket of water and spray on plants.

Snail deterrent: Sprinkle cold fire place ash around vegetables. Snails do not like to crawl across the ash and it's also a simple way of adding potash to your garden. Use un-tannalised wood ash only.

Compost and liquid garden fertilizer: Comfrey leaves added to the compost provide a valuable source of potassium and minerals to activate the compost heap.

Comfrey

Comfrey added to a drum of water makes an excellent liquid fertilizer tea. To this I add seaweed and let it brew.

Refill with water and keep adding more comfrey and seaweed.

Tagetes Minuta and marigolds are excellent plants to clean the soil of eel worms, wireworms, slugs, millipedes and various root-eating pests. Minuta also conquers couch grass, convolvulus and ground ivy, and it enriches the soil. Tagete minuta grows quite tall: plant strategically in troublesome areas, and collect the seeds for future use.

Minuta

Weed-Killer: Place a teaspoon of salt on weeds that are in your lawns, or spray vinegar on them.

Children's Section

Play Dough

1 cup flour

½ cup salt

1 cup water

2 teaspoons food colouring

1 tablespoon vegetable oil

Peppermint essence (optional)

Mix flour and salt. Combine the food colouring, oil and water and add it to the flour. Mould it into dough. Keep in a sealed container in the fridge. This play dough keeps in the fridge for weeks.

Papier Maché glue or glue for children

Mix 1 cup of water with 1 cup of flour. Mix well with a fork until thick and runny.

Stir this into 4 cups of boiling water in a saucepan; simmer for 3 minutes, and leave to cool until warm.

The glue works well when warm; store any leftovers in a container in the fridge and warm them back up again when you need to.

In the garden, children can experiment with making their own soap.

Take a camellia flower, and squeeze it until a soapy slime emerges to create instant fun soap.

Bath Bombs

Herb flowers used must be dry, as moisture will make the bath bombs fizz.

Use dried lavender, chamomile, rose petals or calendula: dry them in the oven by placing them on a baking tray and bake in the oven at 250 degrees for one hour or until dry.

Or place them on an old lace curtain in a dry warm area with air movement for about one week until dry.

3 tablespoons baking soda

1 tablespoon citric acid

8 drops lavender essential oil

1 teaspoon almond or olive oil

Broken flower petals.

Mix altogether, place in a mould, compact tightly, and leave for an hour. Then take out of the mould and watch the children's delight at the sight of a fizzy bath with lots of amazing aromas.

Glossary of Herbs in this book

	Aloe	Aloe vera
	Angelica	Angelica archangelica
	Asparagus	Asparagus officinalis
	Basil	Ocimum basilicum
	Bay	Laurus nobilis
	Borage	Borago
	Carnation	Dianthus
	Catnip	(Catmint) Nepeta cataria
	Chamomile	Chamaemelum nobile
	Chervil	Anthriscus cerefolium
	Chickweed	Stellaria media
	Chicory	Cichorium intybus

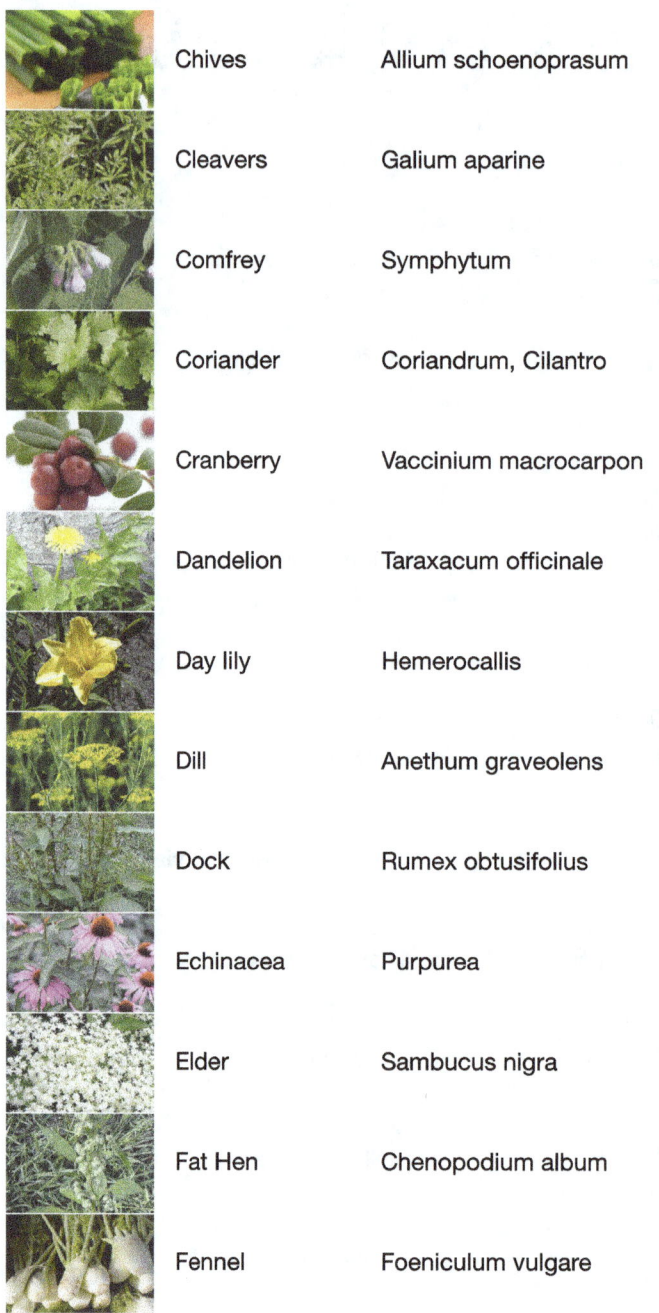

	Chives	Allium schoenoprasum
	Cleavers	Galium aparine
	Comfrey	Symphytum
	Coriander	Coriandrum, Cilantro
	Cranberry	Vaccinium macrocarpon
	Dandelion	Taraxacum officinale
	Day lily	Hemerocallis
	Dill	Anethum graveolens
	Dock	Rumex obtusifolius
	Echinacea	Purpurea
	Elder	Sambucus nigra
	Fat Hen	Chenopodium album
	Fennel	Foeniculum vulgare

Feverfew	Chrysanthemum parthenium
Flaxseed	Linum usitatissimum
Garlic	Allium sativum
Ginger	Zingiber
Ginkgo	Ginkgo biloba
Gladiola	Gladiolus
Hawthorn	Crataegus
Hop	Humulus lupulus
Horseradish	Cochlearia armoracia
Hyssop	Hyssopus officinalis
Lavender	Lavendula Augustifolia
Lemon balm	Melissa officinalis
Lemon Verbena	Aloysia triphylla

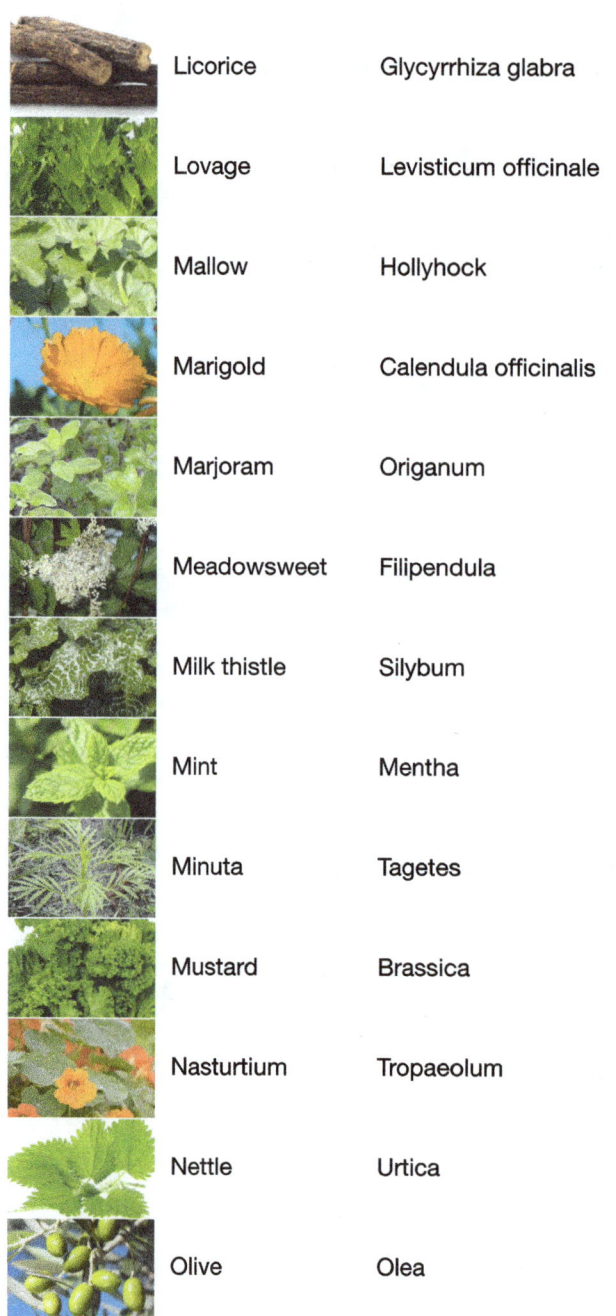

	Licorice	Glycyrrhiza glabra
	Lovage	Levisticum officinale
	Mallow	Hollyhock
	Marigold	Calendula officinalis
	Marjoram	Origanum
	Meadowsweet	Filipendula
	Milk thistle	Silybum
	Mint	Mentha
	Minuta	Tagetes
	Mustard	Brassica
	Nasturtium	Tropaeolum
	Nettle	Urtica
	Olive	Olea

Pansy	Viola
Parsley	Petroselinum
Passion flower	Passiflora incarnata
Pelargonium	Geranium
Pennyroyal	Mentha pulegium
Plantain major	Plantago major
Plantain rib wort	Plantago lanceolate
Rhubarb	Rheum
Rose	Rosa
Rosemary	Rosmarinus officinalis
Sage	Salvia
Salad Burnet	Poterium sanguisorba
Saw palmetto	Serenoa repens

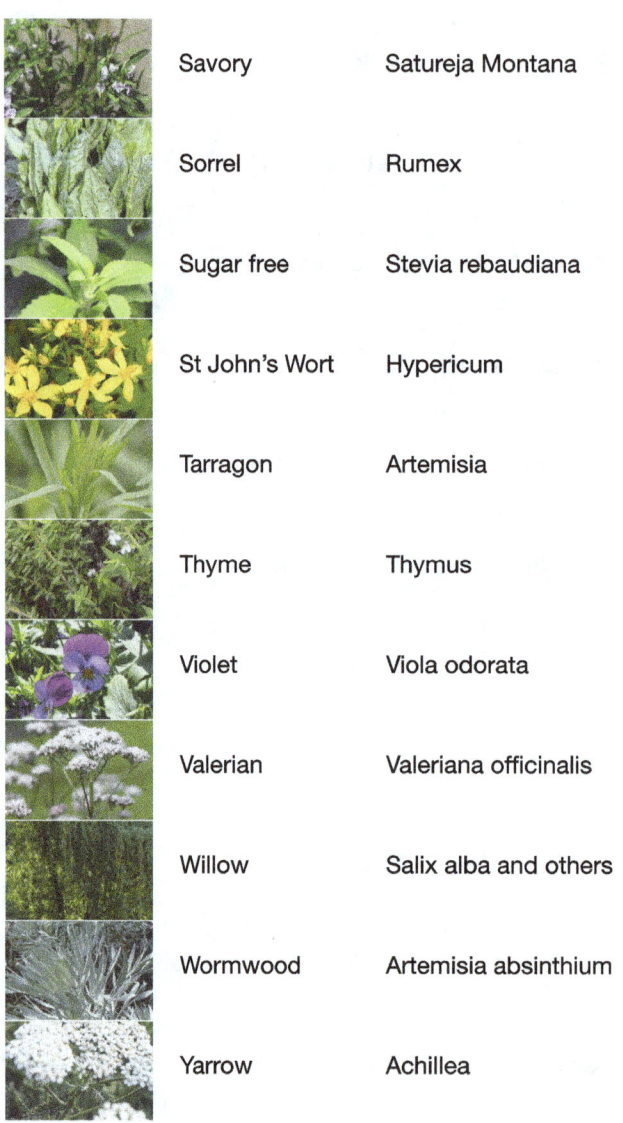

	Savory	Satureja Montana
	Sorrel	Rumex
	Sugar free	Stevia rebaudiana
	St John's Wort	Hypericum
	Tarragon	Artemisia
	Thyme	Thymus
	Violet	Viola odorata
	Valerian	Valeriana officinalis
	Willow	Salix alba and others
	Wormwood	Artemisia absinthium
	Yarrow	Achillea

Conversion Chart

All measurements throughout this book are level and are based on New Zealand measures.

Approximate conversions

Ounces	1	2	3	4	5	6	7	8
Grams	25	50	75	125	150	175	200	225
Ounces	9	10	11	12	13	14	15	16
Grams	250	275	325	350	375	400	450	500

Volumes

1,000ml equals 1 litre equals approx 2 pints

1 metric cup	= 250ml
1 metric teaspoon	= 15ml
1 metric dessertspoon	= 10ml
1 metric teaspoon	= 5ml

Oven Temperature

Thermostatic oven temperatures, reduce temperature from 10 to 25 degrees for thermo wave ovens; generally refer to the book supplied with your oven.

Celsius

130	140	160	180	190	200	215	230	245	260

Fahrenheit

260	290	325	350	375	400	425	450	475	500

Author's note

Suzanne

I was just an ordinary person, living a normal existence - or so I thought - until I had a near-death experience. This experience catapulted me into an incredible new journey.

This put me onto the solid road of the inner spirit; one's very own path to understanding and opening up to the inner-consciousness.

But aside from all of this, my passion is the love of natural products - to teach others about what is around us all. This in turn brought about "Back to Basics": instead of just thinking about writing this book it has come time to put it all on paper.

Even if you learn about only one herb and can pass its amazing properties and qualities onto your children and grandchildren you are passing on the gift of what our Mother Earth provides naturally, and I can say I am blessed in being part of that process.

I delight in sharing my love of teaching "Back to Basics"; I am a motivational speaker on overcoming obstacles and creating a vision and trusting in the inner consciousness of the self.

The universe does not conspire against you. You conspire with the universe by the very thoughts that you put out there.